JEAN-MARIE LECLAIR

THREE ORIGINAL SONATAS

for Two Violins

Op. 3
Nos. 2, 4 & 6

Edited by / Herausgegeben von
Carl Herrmann

VIOLIN I

EIGENTUM DES VERLEGERS · ALLE RECHTE VORBEHALTEN
ALL RIGHTS RESERVED

EDITION PETERS

LONDON · FRANKFURT · LEIPZIG · NEW YORK

CONTENTS / INHALT

Page

Sonata No. 1 (Op. 3, No. 2) 1

Sonata No. 2 (Op. 3, No. 6) 4

Sonata No. 3 (Op. 3, No. 4) 8

SONATE

Violino I

Jean Marie Leclair, Op. 3 No 2
⟨1697 – 1764⟩
Herausgegeben von Carl Herrmann

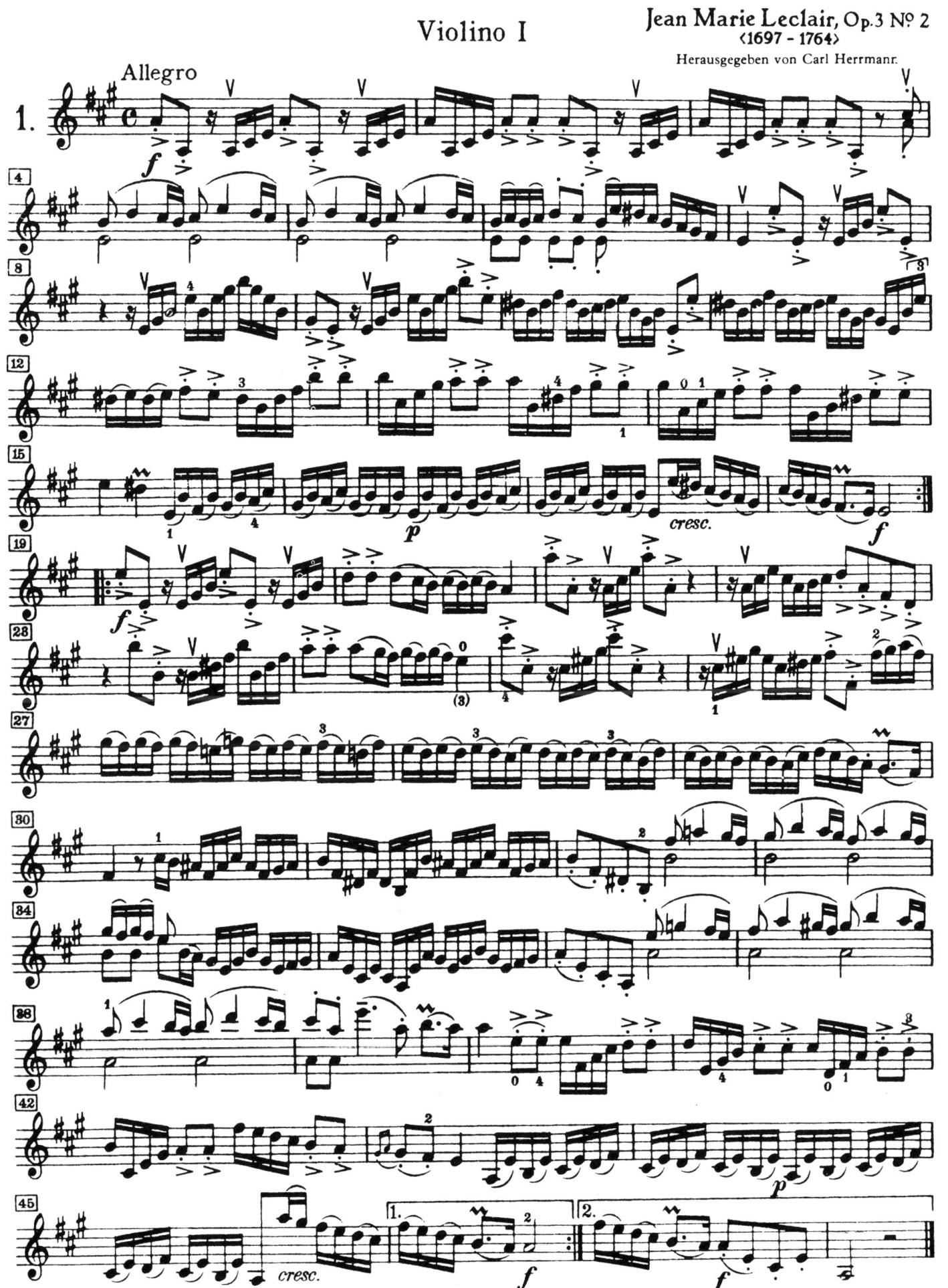

SONATE

Violino I

Op. 3 N.º 6

JEAN-MARIE LECLAIR

THREE ORIGINAL SONATAS
for Two Violins

Op. 3
Nos. 2, 4 & 6

Edited by / Herausgegeben von
Carl Herrmann

VIOLIN II

EIGENTUM DES VERLEGERS · ALLE RECHTE VORBEHALTEN
ALL RIGHTS RESERVED

EDITION PETERS
LONDON · FRANKFURT · LEIPZIG · NEW YORK

CONTENTS / INHALT

Page

Sonata No. 1 (Op. 3, No. 2) 1

Sonata No. 2 (Op. 3, No. 6) 4

Sonata No. 3 (Op. 3, No. 4) 8

SONATE

Violino II

Jean Marie Leclair, Op. 3 No. 2
⟨1697 – 1764⟩
Herausgegeben von Carl Herrmann

Edition Peters No. 7786

© Copyright 2005 by Hinrichsen Edition, Peters Edition Ltd, London

Violino II

SONATE

Op. 3 N° 6

Violino II

SONATE

Violino II

Op. 3 N° 4

GIGA

Allegro moderato

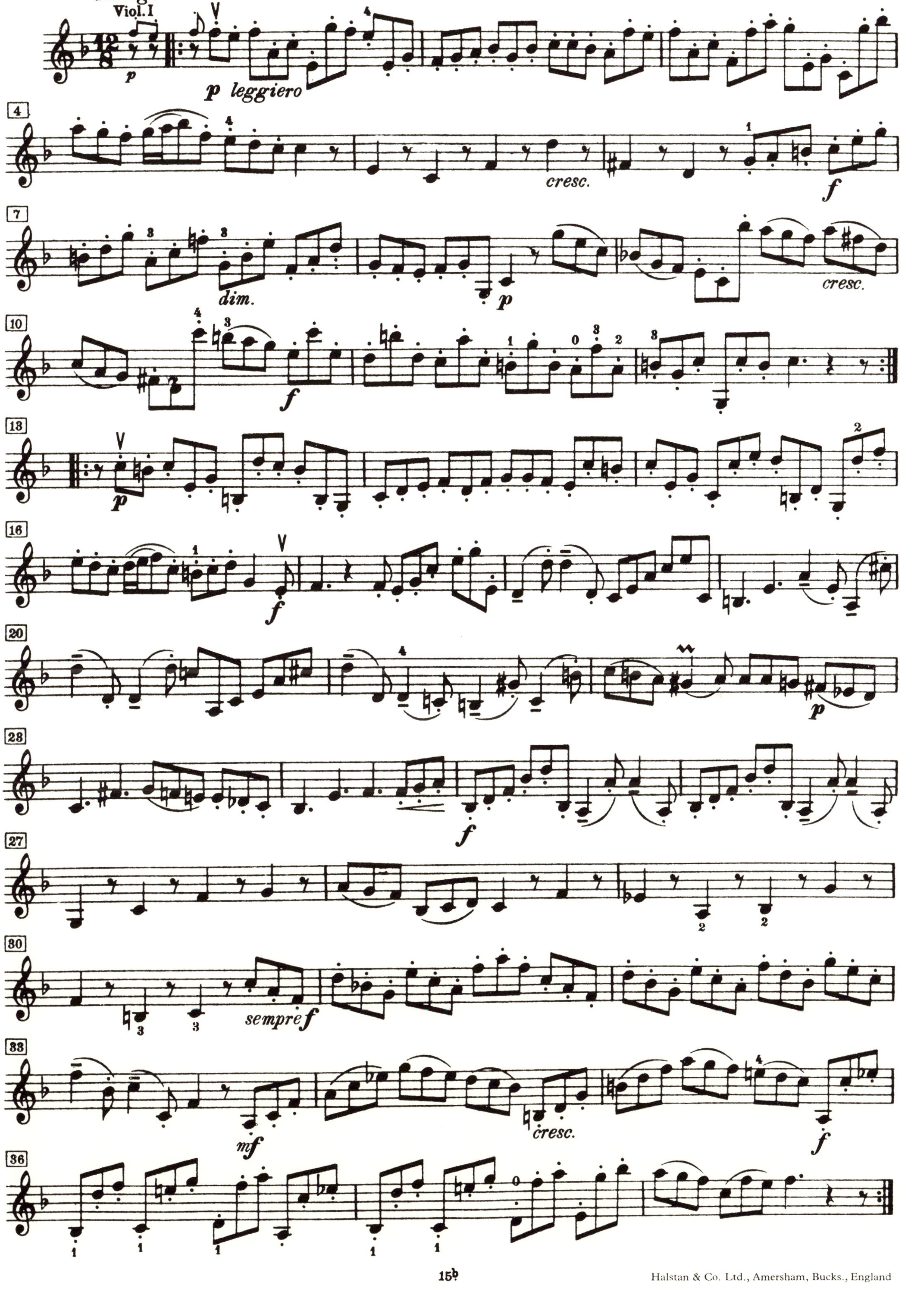

Halstan & Co. Ltd., Amersham, Bucks., England

SONATE

Violino I

Op. 3 No. 4

Allegro assai

Violino I